The Way of Love

CISTERCIAN PUBLICATIONS INC.

Kalamazoo, Michigan 49008

1977

The Way of Love is number 16 in the Cistercian Fathers Series

© 1976 Photographs, Brother Patrick Hart

© 1976 Text, Cistercian Publications, Inc.
1749 W. Michigan Avenue—W.M.U.
Kalamazoo, Michigan 49008

Available in Great Britain and Europe from

A. R. Mowbray & Co Ltd
Osney Mead
Oxford OX2 0EG

ISBN 0-87907-616-X (casebound)
ISBN 0-87907-966-5 (paper)

Typeset at Humble Hills Graphics; Kalamazoo, Michigan 49004
Printed in the United States of America

Friends, let us love one another,
  for love comes from God
and everyone who loves is begotten by God
and knows God.
Anyone who does not love can never have known God,
for God is love.

I John 4:7–9

*The beginning of love
is choice.*

AELRED OF RIEVAULX
The Mirror of Charity 3:24

*The affection of love
is a delicate plant . . .*

GILBERT OF HOYLAND
On the Song of Songs, 11:1

*Love is solid. It may be fretted by annoyance,
but it simply cannot be worn away.*

JOHN OF FORD
On the Song of Songs, 11:4

Love is the fountain of life,
and the soul which does not drink from it
cannot be called alive.

BERNARD OF CLAIRVAUX
Precept and Dispensation, 60

Nothing in life is happier than to love faithfully and to be loved in return.

ADAM OF PERSEIGNE
Letter 3:39

*If love is not whole-hearted,
it is not whole.*

BERNARD OF CLAIRVAUX
On the Song of Songs, 18:3

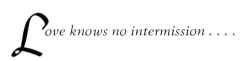

Love knows no intermission . . . .

JOHN OF FORD
On the Song of Songs, 2:1

*Love touches us
spontaneously
and it makes us
spontaneous.*

BERNARD OF CLAIRVAUX
On Loving God, 16

*The treasure of our love
is hidden in the field
of our heart
and lies
buried down
in its very depths.*

JOHN OF FORD
On the Song of Songs, 13:4

Let your love be strong and constant,
neither giving in to fear nor cowering at hard work.
Let us love affectionately, discreetly, intensely.

BERNARD OF CLAIRVAUX
On the Song of Songs, 20:4

*L*ove is like gold: if you hammer at it, you broaden it. *If you strike it, you do not cut but lengthen it.*
If you persist in striking it, it also persists in increasing.

JOHN OF FORD
On the Song of Songs, 11:4

*True love deserves its reward,
it does not demand it.*

BERNARD OF CLAIRVAUX
On Loving God, 17

*L*ove seeks with tenderness,
finds with gladness,
enjoys with blessedness,
and is fulfilled.

ADAM OF PERSEIGNE
Letter 3:20

In love there is no lord, no servant:
for love excludes all exercise of lordship . . . .

The Life of Lutgarde of Aywières

*Love and humility
grow together.*

JOHN OF FORD
On the Song of Songs, 3:4

*L*ove and humility
have more in common
than love and majesty.

GILBERT OF HOYLAND
On the Song of Songs, 3

A heart once truly seized by love is no longer at its own disposal.

BERNARD OF
CLAIRVAUX
Letter 74

*True love . . .
has its reward:
the object of its love.*

BERNARD OF
CLAIRVAUX
On Loving God, 17

If we love the beautiful, you are the beauty of all that is beautiful.
If we love the good, you are the goodness of all that is good.

WILLIAM OF ST THIERRY
On the Song of Songs, 54

Love's birthplace is God. There it is born, there it is nourished, there it is reared. There it is at home, not a tourist, but a native. For by God alone is love given and in him it endures . . . .

WILLIAM OF ST THIERRY
The Nature and Dignity of Love, 5

*The love of God is a river of peace,
    streaming out in its greatness and flowing in with gentle waters.
At the same time it is a torrent, rushing along with mighty force
and sweeping everything away with it.*

JOHN OF FORD
On the Song of Songs, 13:4

God's love is to our love,
to our natural affections,
as our soul is to our body.
If it is in it, it is alive . . . .

WILLIAM OF ST THIERRY
The Mirror of Faith, 65

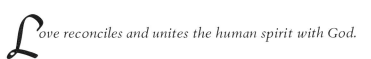

*L*ove reconciles and unites the human spirit with God.

GILBERT OF HOYLAND
On the Song of Songs, 11

ℽou loved us first so that we might love you.
And this was not because you needed to be loved
by us, but because we could not be what you created us
to be unless we loved you.

WILLIAM OF ST THIERRY
Contemplating God, 10

*The most compelling motive for loving God
is surely that he shines forth like light,
making himself perceptible and a joy.*

ISAAC OF STELLA
Sermon 24:18

God is the reason for loving God.

BERNARD OF CLAIRVAUX
On Loving God, 22

Love is God, and no created thing can satisfy a person made to the image of God except God who is love.

BERNARD OF CLAIRVAUX
On the Song of Songs, 18:6

The love of God is born in man by grace, fed with the milk of reading, nourished with the food of meditation, strengthened and enlightened by prayer.

WILLIAM OF ST THIERRY
The Golden Epistle, 171

To believe in him is to go to him by loving him.

WILLIAM OF ST THIERRY
The Mirror of Faith, 43

The person who loves God is with God to the extent that he loves.

BERNARD OF CLAIRVAUX
Precept and Dispensation, 60

*G*od loved us first,
　　not with an affective
but an effective love.

WILLIAM OF ST THIERRY
The Enigma of Faith, 90

'*Not that we loved God,*
*but that he loved us.' (*I John 4:10*)*
He loved us even before we existed,
and he loved us when we resisted him.

BERNARD OF CLAIRVAUX
On the Song of Songs, 20:2

From the fullness of joy the Father utters
the whole of himself to the Son,
and in the same way the Son, together with the Father,
utters the whole of himself to the Holy Spirit,
so that these three are one single font of love.

JOHN OF FORD
On the Song of Songs, 14:4

The love of God, God who is love, the Holy Spirit,
   pours himself into our love and our spirit
and attracts us to himself.
Then God loves himself in us
and makes us, our spirit and our love,
one with himself.

WILLIAM OF ST THIERRY
The Golden Epistle, 170

How much better does someone see God who loves God.

JOHN OF FORD
On the Song of Songs, 11:3

Many people have said many things about God, but who can speak about him except himself? Only love, enlightened love speaking inwardly to God, is capable of doing it.

WILLIAM OF ST THIERRY
The Mirror of Faith, 75

*B*efore pure prayer can be uttered,
　　it must always be anticipated
by the spirit of love,
for that is what utters it,
sets its incense burning,
and directs its smoke.

JOHN OF FORD
On the Song of Songs, 12:1

To love God is to know him.
Unless he is loved,
he is not known.
And unless he is known,
he is not loved.
He is known to the degree that he is loved,
and he is loved to the degree that he is known.

WILLIAM OF ST THIERRY
On the Song of Songs, 76

Learn to love tenderly,
to love wisely,
to love courageously:
tenderly so we are not lured away,
wisely so we do not stumble away,
courageously, so we are not pushed away
from the love of the Lord.

BERNARD OF CLAIRVAUX
On the Song of Songs, 20:4

*Each and every kind of love
reveals some small resemblance
to that true and everlasting love,
if anyone takes the trouble
to look for it.*

JOHN OF FORD
On the Song of Songs, 14:5

*The most important thing of all to seek is the love of God,
which is the beginning and the end of everything.
As a result of this we may also become worthy of being loved by men.
And by striving to grow in God's love,
we may learn what to do with men's.*

GUERRIC OF IGNY
Sermon 24:4

*N*o one can possibly love in God
who does not love God first.
We must love God first
so that then we can
love our neighbor in God.

BERNARD OF CLAIRVAUX
On Loving God, 25

*Who can love another person
if he does not love himself?*

AELRED OF RIEVAULX
Spiritual Friendship 3:128

*H*ow can we love our neighbor unconditionally,
if we do not love him in God?

BERNARD OF CLAIRVAUX
On Loving God, 25

*J*ust as God loves himself in us and we have learned to love in ourselves only God, so we begin to love our neighbor as ourselves.

For in our neighbor we love God . . . .

WILLIAM OF ST THIERRY
Contemplating God, 12

*W*e cannot love God without our neighbor or our neighbor without God.

GUERRIC OF IGNY
Sermon 24:4

*L**ove is chaste when it seeks the beloved person and not something of his.*

BERNARD OF CLAIRVAUX
On the Song of Songs, 7:3

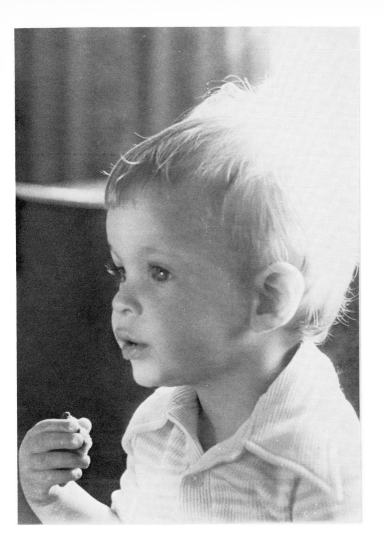

*L*ove is the fountain and source of friendship.
There can be love without friendship,
but friendship without love is impossible.

AELRED OF RIEVAULX
Spiritual Friendship, 3:2

*If someone you love offends you,
continue to love him despite the hurt.
His conduct may compel the withdrawal
of friendship, but never of love.*

AELRED OF RIEVAULX
Spiritual Friendship, 3:44

Every human bond serves love's cause,
whether in the relationship of parents to children or children to parents,
whether in the deeper and closer relationship of a husband to his wife
or a wife to her husband,
whether in any one of all the various relationships that make up human society.
In all of these, love attracts them either to advance
or to strive to advance
toward a simple principle of unity.

JOHN OF FORD
On the Song of Songs, 14:5

Unity consists in singleness of love . . . .

BERNARD OF CLAIRVAUX
Apologia, 8

here is no dwelling together in unity
except in love . . . .

GILBERT OF HOYLAND
On the Song of Songs, 11

Let love overcome shyness. Let affection drive out fear . . . .

AELRED OF RIEVAULX
Letter to his Sister, 31

The person who loves never lacks confidence,
  knowing that he whom hearts cannot deceive
loves everyone who loves him,
even when he reproves and corrects them.

GUERRIC OF IGNY
Sermon 23:4

Holy love is accompanied by great confidence.

GILBERT OF HOYLAND
On the Song of Songs, 3

If I do not love, I do not hope. Nor do I love unless I hope.

WILLIAM OF ST THIERRY
Meditation, 9:10

As he in his love for us went to the limit of love, so we should—if possible— love him without any limit.

WILLIAM OF ST THIERRY
The Golden Epistle, 230

'*Love is strong as death.*' (Song of Songs, 8:6)
Since, by the power of his love, God's strength
has been made weak to death,
love is no longer strong as death,
but stronger than death.

GUERRIC OF IGNY
Sermon 41:3

*When at last we arrive at the end toward which we are striving . . .
love will not only exist, it will be perfect,
because what we now love by hoping and believing,
we shall then love by seeing and possessing.*

WILLIAM OF ST THIERRY
The Mirror of Faith, 1

The texts in *The Way of Love* were written by cistercian monks who lived in France and England during the twelfth century. Their name, 'cistercian', comes from the cistern, or spring, found at their first home, Cîteaux.

The Cistercians sought to express their love for God and their fellow men by living in simplicity, by discarding everything which might come between themselves and their Creator, and by disentangling themselves from the web of society. They possessed only the necessities of life. They cleared their own land and raised their own food. They turned away from elaborate ceremonies and intricate arguments to search for God in Scripture, in their own being, and in their brothers. They relied on experience more than analysis to learn ever more deeply to love God, self, creation, and one another.

One of the early monks wrote of their way of life:

> *Our order is an awareness of our need.*
> *It is humbleness.*
> *It is poverty, freely accepted,*
> *obedience, peace,*
> *joy in the Holy Spirit . . .*

> *Our order means learning to be silent,*
> *to fast, to keep watch, to pray,*
> *to work with our hands*
> *and, above all, to cling to that most excellent way*
> *which is*
> *love.*

The works of the early Cistercians are available in English translation in the Cistercian Fathers Series (CF) from

CISTERCIAN PUBLICATIONS INC.
1749 W. Michigan Avenue—WMU
Kalamazoo, Michigan 49008

A. R. MOWBRAY & CO. LTD.
Osney Mead
Oxford OX2 0EG

TEXT SOURCES

Cistercian Fathers (CF) Volume Number

ADAM OF PERSEIGNE (+1221)
    Letters I — CF 21

AELRED OF RIEVAULX (+1167)
    A Letter to his Sister (Rule for a Recluse) — CF 2
    The Mirror of Charity — in preparation
    Spiritual Friendship — CF 5

BERNARD OF CLAIRVAUX (+1153)
    Apologia to Abbot William — CF 1
    Five Books on Consideration — CF 37*
    Letters — in preparation
    On Loving God — CF 13
    Precept and Dispensation — CF 1
    Sermons on the Song of Songs — CF 4*, 7* & others in preparation

GILBERT OF HOYLAND (+1172)
    Sermons on the Song of Songs — in preparation

GUERRIC OF IGNY (+1157)
    Liturgical Sermons — CF 8 & 32

ISAAC OF STELLA (+1169)
    Sermons for the Liturgical Year — in preparation

JOHN OF FORD (+1220)
    Sermons on the Song of Songs — CF 29* & others in preparation

LUTGARDE OF AYWIERES' Life — projected

WILLIAM OF ST THIERRY (+1148)
    Contemplating God — CF 3
    The Enigma of Faith — CF 9
    Exposition on the Song of Songs — CF 6
    The Golden Epistle — CF 12*
    Meditations — CF 3
    The Mirror of Faith — in preparation
    The Nature and Dignity of Love — in preparation

available in paper as well as case binding

Photographs by BROTHER PATRICK HART

Texts selected by ROZANNE ELDER

Book design by GALE AKINS

Typefaces in book: THOMPSON QUILLSCRIPT *display*
ALDINE ROMAN (IBM version of 'Bembo') *text*

A NOTE ON THE PHOTOGRAPHS

The camera I used, a Canon FX, was the same camera which John Howard Griffin had given Thomas Merton on a long-term loan. After Merton's death in Bangkok, the camera was found among his personal effects and returned to Gethsemani. Mr Griffin felt that the camera should remain at Gethsemani, and through his encouragement and patient instruction I began photographing simple things of life, details of rock texture, trees, flowers, and so many things we see each day and take for granted. I've tried to use it as a contemplative instrument, much as Griffin and Merton have done.

Brother Patrick Hart

†

We are grateful for the advice and help of Margaret Hooper, Sue Beckett, Ann French, Harvey Simmonds, Marylee and Carl Mitcham and the cistercian monks of Ava and Gethsemani.